Celebrating the Family Name of Rice

Walter the Educator

Silent King Books
a WhichHead Entertainment Imprint

Copyright © 2024 by Walter the Educator

All rights reserved. No part of this book may be reproduced in any manner whatsoever without written permission except in the case of brief quotations embodied in critical articles and reviews.

First Printing, 2024

Disclaimer

This book is a literary work; the story is not about specific persons, locations, situations, and/or circumstances unless mentioned in a historical context. Any resemblance to real persons, locations, situations, and/or circumstances is coincidental. This book is for entertainment and informational purposes only. The author and publisher offer this information without warranties expressed or implied. No matter the grounds, neither the author nor the publisher will be accountable for any losses, injuries, or other damages caused by the reader's use of this book. The use of this book acknowledges an understanding and acceptance of this disclaimer.

CELEBRATING THE FAMILY NAME OF RICE

Celebrating the Family Name of Rice is a memory book that belongs to the Celebrating Family Name Book Series by Walter the Educator. Collect them all and more books at WaltertheEducator.com

USE THE EXTRA SPACE TO DOCUMENT YOUR FAMILY MEMORIES THROUGHOUT THE YEARS

ID
RICE

Beneath a sky of silver hue,

The name of Rice, both strong and true,

Was born from earth, from root, from seed,

A tale of honor, grit, and creed.

Through winding hills and fields of green,

Where rivers carve a path serene,

The name has flowed like water's grace,

Enduring time, in every place.

In ages past, when soil was tilled,

The hands of Rice with strength were filled,

They sowed with care, they reaped with pride,

In every furrow, dreams would bide.

The family name, a thread of gold,

Wove stories rich, untamed, untold,

In every heart, a steadfast fire,

To rise and reach, to never tire.

They built their homes with stone and song,

Each brick a note, both fierce and strong,

Their laughter echoed, wild and free,

Through generations, endlessly.

The name of Rice, a banner high,

That reached the earth, yet kissed the sky,

With roots that run in sacred ground,

Yet soar where only dreams are found.

A name that whispers to the wind,

Of all the places it has been,

From quiet shores to bustling towns,

The Rice name wears its earthly crowns.

For in each soul who bears this name,

There lies a spark, an ancient flame,

A love of land, a heart that's kind,

A will that's bright, a brilliant mind.

Through trials fierce and shadows long,

The Rice name sings its steadfast song,

Unyielding through the storm's embrace,

Yet softened by its quiet grace.

In every hand, a tender touch,

To heal, to build, to love so much,

In every voice, a gentle tone,

That turns a house into a home.

ABOUT THE CREATOR

Walter the Educator is one of the pseudonyms for Walter Anderson. Formally educated in Chemistry, Business, and Education, he is an educator, an author, a diverse entrepreneur, and he is the son of a disabled war veteran. "Walter the Educator" shares his time between educating and creating. He holds interests and owns several creative projects that entertain, enlighten, enhance, and educate, hoping to inspire and motivate you. Follow, find new works, and stay up to date with Walter the Educator™

at WaltertheEducator.com

Milton Keynes UK
Ingram Content Group UK Ltd.
UKHW051141031124
450424UK00019B/1090